BLK
N
WHT

A Collection of Poems

Gwendolyn Jackson

ISBN: 978-1-7324191-1-7

BLK N WHT/Jackson-1st ed.

1. Poems. 2. Poetry. 3. Verse.
4. Jackson 5. Female Perspective
6. African American Perspective   7. Christian Belief

NFB Publishing/Amelia Press
<<<>>>
119 Dorchester Road
Buffalo, New York 14213
For more information please visit
nfbpublishing.com

Dedication:

To the loves I lost and found and
the ones who chose to stay around

Contents

Introduction

Ever had a moment when whatever you tried just did not work or it was not enough to handle the situation and no matter what you did, the problem remained somewhat unfixable? Well, let me encourage you with a few little words of wisdom and some inspirational droplets of pearls that no matter what life say cannot be done – the battle is already won.

Hello and greetings to all who are waiting for the moment of their release, that if you hang in there just a little while longer, a mighty breakthrough will explode right in your face. Now what does this have to do with things being Black and White?

This book of poems is just a little more revealing into my life and perhaps into yours concerning some real feelings pondered and considered as we walk the road of Christian living yet still having to deal with life and what it brings and takes away. We are still human and have the challenges of being in this earthly realm but please do not think I am giving you any reason to succumb to its defeating tactics but to overcome with the anointing power given you from the beginning – not yours but the Word's.

Take some time to be encouraged, inspired, uplifted, motivated, and stirred on by the sayings of this book and hopefully to share with others. It is my privilege to serve and my honor to be chosen for such a task as this.

PRAISE MY LORD AND SAVIOR JESUS CHRIST

Gwendolyn Jackson

A Clean Slate

A new year starts with a new day

Sometimes it can start with a new moment

A door is shut closed another cracks open

An old habit is released a hand let loose

Not grasping for old and familiar

For the slate is wiped clean

Even the chalk residue blown away

A smile on the face of the freed one

There a twinkle in the eye

Pep in the step

The debt is forgiven

All weights are lifted

It is not a begin over, it is a begin anew

Like a path of fresh snow never traveled

Journey will lead into the untried

The slate is clean

Am I Enough?

There are so many things you manage to put in MY place

If I could be the first one you acknowledge in your haste

This and that so much of life and more life things still

Doing what I would like and not what you may feel

Not second or even third but first in line for real

When the trials are too much can you think to kneel

Ever making ME the enough that can fill your time

But enough for this period with the right decisions being Mine

Putting aside all the world's opinions or what they may say

For what really matter is done for ME and will be done MY way

This would be the task or assignment to be done in MY name

Filling in the blanks of your life just like the purpose I came

Who and what is more important and does it carry more weight

The way this world is going it must not think much is at stake

I can be the enough to fill the voids pain has left in your heart

Filing them in completely, wholly, fully not just a piece or a part

Being the real thing not giving the world's fake and phony crud

But the genuine undeniable fulfilling more than enough lastly love

Enough for you can be more than even what you will imagine or think

If you will let MY heart be the only heart to bond with yours in sync

Am I Enough Continued

Us doing as YOU have directed obedience to YOU is my purpose and goal

Knowing what YOU sacrificed YOUR life to save and redeem my immoral soul

This is the question I was asked; can I be enough more than anything else

Yes, I want YOU to be my all and all with loving YOU more than myself

A Noise in the Camp

There is a noise in the camp

Those without can hear

Rumbling so loud overpowering the air

Puzzling and confusing the enemy to fear

A sound that says the Victor is here

They know that sound, the one of jubilee

Heard that sound before, the one of victory

The sound released to all when the battle won

Too soon for that when war is not finished or done

Send it up in advance; send it up because His is around

Knowing what can happen yet triumph not found

There is a noise in the camp

Ringing through the mountains in each valley

In the course of defeat still possible to rally

Lifting and compelling the standard up higher

In front of the foe hurting but must not tire

Attacked on every side shield and buckler in place

Defending what is true sincerely with haste

Let the praise come first let it sound the alarm

When He is in the midst, there will be no harm

But the yet praise is the test, endurance is the grade

The battle will not take away from the victory made

There is a noise in the camp

All in A Day

The change can happen suddenly all in one day

All the seasons splendor wondrously in their way

The flowers bloom yet there are no leaves on the trees

The sun heats the ground yet there's a cool breeze

Where is the place that's noted for a sudden storm?

But in two days the snow has almost melted it's gone

It's my place which has recreated itself again brand new

The place I was born some said we just couldn't do

What I love are the green spaces made for our advantage

More than one in every neighborhood beautifully managed

Our parks are legendary copied by other cities our style

Colors of the rainbow can be seen for miles and miles

You see we are mostly outdoor people even when it's cold

The warmth brings the wanderlust spirit we just can't hold

Four seasons is the norm it's what we are accustomed to

This is about my hometown Buffalo, NY

Almost All the Time

What should you look for?
In a potential relationship
A mate you want to be with
Almost all the time
My theory is this
If you can find someone that
Answers most of your desires
With only a little to work on
Grab hold of them
They could be the one that
Puts a smile on your face
From the mere thought of them
Quickness in your step
When it is time to go home
Laughter in your voice
After hearing theirs
A gleam in your eye from
Just a glimpse of their face
You just want to be with them
Almost all the time
Always!

Belief

*I*f you can believe, the sun is going to rise and set everyday

Why can't you believe God's promise for you?

If you can believe, there are mansions in heaven

Why can't you believe the things

God promised you here on earth

Believe for the ministry, the husband,

The wife, the financial increase

Believe that God will exalt you for His Glory

When we lift Him up above the earth (John 12:32)

He draws us along with Him (Rom 8:17)

If you can believe, things won't work out

Just because you do not see it

Why not believe things will work out when you cannot see it?

Do not be so quick to believe the negative

When the positive is just as easy to believe

When there is a choice between the two

Whose report will you believe?

I will believe the report of the Lord

Brand New

To be transformed made free from sin

Now renewed, now reborn, safe again

Reshaped, transfigured, molded into

The image of Christ, His will I will do

Levels, realms, new heights perceived

Eyes opened, mind refreshed, anointing received

Helmet, sword, shield all in place

Prepared for the goal - Heaven - His face

Create the Conversion

We can make the transition that's in us

Life will help with some of it that's life

Things do happen that makes us do

They will make us assess the direction we go

Either left or right or forward or back

Life has a way of starting or stopping

But the Lord has His way of making it

For the good, the correct, the stable, for love

Let's not fear change or the move or the shift

Be flexible with the conversion that makes it

Worth the evolution, the development, the switch

His plan our move

Do You Mind

I am a truth-seeker with many illuminating thoughts to my credit

Much of life experience and circumstances I feel I have to edit

Relationships that have gone by the wayside moments, time relived

Reworked restructured fine-tuned much thought I must give

You see this is real life stuff and I have to tell how I feel

Full blow conversations beautiful words that no one will ever hear

The fact that I live alone have enhanced my skill of witty thought

Mentally expressing the angry, hurt and love casted aside answers sought

Into the scenario is the realism of having loved only one time before

Believing that love is love no matter who is surrendering not less but more

From start to finish in a few minutes, a relationship can run its course

The head has reasoned it out with an unprotected heart receiving the worse

Remember what I said before the minds conversation can tell the truth

Silently over and over not aloud for the mouth is always mute

You see we as women should always remember to treat ourselves as queens

Being careful and not accepting nor having and wanting just any old thing

Do You Mind Continued

Silently working it out thinking and working it again out for the better

Leaving no detail out remember every situation each one to the letter

Head banter one ear to the other mind seriously voices it needs to be said

Regaining what was lost in time with effort making sure the point made

We are what God made us loving creatures giving all we're made to care

Wanting to say it so the world can hear how a soul and heart will dare

Here is the question again once more the question is Do You Mind?

The answer yes, we mind, mindfully mentally seek for release almost all the time

Fascination

What is this fascination with time and why?
Always aware although it slips by
Making me march to the tick of the clock
My mind, my body caught in its lock
Does not like good strides in its grip
Not in my favor always, it seems to slip
Wish sometimes could turn it back
Redo all those things that I let lack
Cannot make up but forge ahead
Wait it will not, so flow with it instead
Blessed is the one that takes her time
Lesson learned with a stable mind
The key is endurance time is open to
Those who chase the Maker eternity pursue
Listen to what is spoken but hear what is said
Heard what was meant unspoken words dread
Time will tell the end from the beginning
Will reveal if this is the fifth or ninth inning
The day will come when time is over for good
Then all this time fascination revealed and understood

Free Hand

What is love when given without asking?
Received without paying it back
Love is pure and without conditions
Time is taking its time
Life is giving its life
Second upon second
Moments flow into moments
When will time evolve into the second
that the moment fulfilled?
Going through the motion of one step at a time
There's that word again. Time
Told about season - growth planted- sown and reaped
What season will the harvest be realized?
Realization is that time will not be rushed
Season may come and go
Life will still be lived
Harvest in its due time
That word again. Time
Scary thoughts
Will my time ever come on this side of time?
Make time while time is now
Eternity has no time but life
Time will not bend or adjust to fit the moment
The moment. The moment will just have to fit

Fringes

Fingers still lingering trying to hold on

Wanting to hold tight still trying to grip

Memories are all that are left

Even that needs to fade away

What are you doing there - words ring in the ear

Shouldn't ever be there never really invited

Allowed along the fringes attached to nothing

Kept hanging on with no chance of being whole

No more tears, no more trying

Wasting time never will be valid

Real love hurts the pain is for real

Heart pitter-patters heart now still

End will come just prolonged

No one will say this is the end

Keeping the string loose but still intact

Nudging ever so gently choking out life

Must be released this time, this time it is fine

Gave My Children

Yesterday I gave them courage

Today I gave them strength

I have shown my children God

He Knows Your Scent

*H*e knows your scent ,you know that scent you wear

He knows your scent, the one that says you are near

A subtle whiff that enter the room before you are there

Just a hint of fragrance chosen with purposed care

That sweet odor embedded deep within your pores

Released in the atmosphere for the one you adore

With a turn of your head, your hair carries it too

With every movement, every motion in all that you do

Preparation made, details done so true

Seeking to catch the attention of the one, you want to woo

Now what is the scent we all wear for all of our life?

It is the scent of praise rising up in the midst of strife

Well pleasing and desired above all the sacrifice of praise

Whatever it takes, what is suffered that scent we will raise

Through trials and struggle the fragrance become intense

Becoming sweeter greater overpowering the sense

There is another scent another scent he knows

That is the one of sin an odor that he deploys

The stench that is offence to his nose

For the love of Him, let us not send it up any more

Let us send a scent of righteousness for our soul's sake

Showing how we cherish the sacrifices, he makes

Who is the man who knows your scent so well?

He Knows Your Scent Continued

Who is the man who knows my scent from yours I will tell
He is the one that carries you through troubles and prevails
The one who cares enough to hold you even if you fail
He is the one for whom the attraction seems to be so strong
The one and only one for whom our spirit desires and long
The one to whom our scent of praise is released
To the one called Jesus Christ our praise sacrifice is pleased

He Said He Would

Who would be the one for this daunting mission
Other names said but all came up lacking
A great sacrifice had to be made
He said he would with God's backing
In the beginning was the word
He was the beginning
From the start the plan was made
He said He would be our sin ending
From the womb of a virgin He came
She was chosen and agreed with the plan
He said he would be born to die no cause
For the human to live and succeed be redeemed
The progression took all of thirty- three years
Heal, deliver, salvation shedding of blood and tears
Purpose was to save and exchange one life for others
Then the ultimate sacrifice His life was given
With whips He was beaten but still He was living
The Word said He would suffer the indignities of the cross
The Word said He would to save a world that was lost
He said if He was lifted up above the earth He would draw
A sin sick world with its many imperfections and flaws
This had to be done for us to be forgiven if we would just ask
The word went beneath the earth and back His final task
He said He would die His purpose and be risen again
For it is written He said He would sacrifice His life for our sin
Don't let what He said He would do be in vain for your soul
Put the Word in your mind, body and heart and let it make you whole

Heart Decision

I heard somewhere that the best decisions come from the heart

But I thought those decisions were too emotional.

The best ones should come from the head being

They would be the most reasonable so you would think

But I discovered the ones from the head will have me doing nothing

Because it is the most sensible and a little cold.

With the heart man believes unto righteousness

And also flows the issues of life. What does this mean?

I will stop trying to figure things out based on my information

And trust God with all my heart that

He will make the best decision concerning me, one of His children.

Thank you for the LOVE.

The story touched my heart and you have too.

So I have decided to have a mind like Christ and a heart full of Him too

Hold Fast

Hold fast to all you hear for the spirit is speaking unto the church
Keep all My sayings in your heart for the enemy is on his search
Hold fast to the peace for My life was sacrificed for your good
Maintaining all that you have already learned and understood
Don't get weary in well doing but preserve all the good you are taught
Looking to the author and finisher of your faith with all aforethought
Letting go of the pretense of being either hot or cold not one or the other
Possessing what was given which is the strength a word of faith to utter
A true worshipper not talking about being judged if you are not in sin
Doing what's your reasonable service that is expected for a good end
Hold fast to the principles proven for your soul to prosper and succeed
To spread the good word to a world that is so greatly in need
Hold fast to righteous fundamentals that are instilled in you from the start
Not to your own understanding but hold fast to the
Word that is God's heart

Inspired by the writings from my late husband, Leon

I Know Where It Is

You think I do not but I do

I know you cannot see what is right in front of you

My hand is on it or it is within my reach

Perfectly organized to my satisfaction you may have to seek

The piles are on the chairs and cabinets they are stacked

Even on my desktop, I have them packed

Had many an offer to straight and clean

Used every spot even the wall my stuff leans

Did you come to see my mess or it is I you need?

Uncomfortable in my domain then leave here indeed

My stay is only temporary, this is not my home

Still got my work done but now I am gone

Worked well to the best of my ability at my own pace

Will you think my messy desk or the smile that came easily to my face?

It's the smile that we all remember and the graceful strides of his walk

His quiet nature and let us just get it done talk

If you ever met Mark, an impression was made

Impressed with a kinship that will last for all of your days

This poem is dedicated to Mark Hart, a friend and co-worker upon hearing of his death but remembering the part of his life I shared.

In The Morning

$\mathcal{H}$ear my voice in the morning, my prayers to Your ear

No matter what may come or go my voice will You hear

For You are with me through the dark of my storm

You will lift me up over and above the enemy's swarm

Even when dreams want the night terrors to bring me hurt

The thoughts of the morning light are the only thoughts to insert

The light of Your love alone will chase the darkness away

No matter what the hour, midnight hour could be my day

Because the bright and morning star is who You say is You

Even in Your darkest hour on the cross still the light shone through

My tears have a time limit, not always limited will be their fall

For in the morning light, You're there to wipe not one but them all

Inspired by some writings from my late husband, Leon.

Ins and Outs

Looking for people to see the inside of me

Because God knows the ins and outs of me

Waiting for people to see the transparency that's me

But God knows the ins and outs of me

Waiting for people to see what they can't see in me

Looking for those that may feel the pain in me

Wanting to reveal what I really truly feel

But God still knows the ins and outs that's me

Maybe I should not look or wait for what people might see

Because God knows what He has put in me

It's You

Good morning Lord

Thank you for this day

Rain, clouds, fog, sunshine and all

Still have a chance to get everything right

Praising your name for all you are

This is for you my life dedicated to you

Living it with you loving in you

Jesus it is you

Good night Lord

Let It Rip

Some of us wear the old garment with pockets full of past regret

Making patches with the new threads not able to set

Time to remove it get rid of it for its time is past tense

The look is not at its best even gives off a slight stench

The lining is hanging off the bottom it really looks a mess

A quick fix is to pull only one thread but will it hold is the test

Buttons missing here and there but were they missing before

The garment was already torn but now it is torn even more

Wearing two garments makes them both feel too tight

Movement is restricted but still trying to close them with all might

If the old is what you cling to it would fit and fit well

One arm in one sleeve with the other hanging by a nail

A nail why a nail does it has any significance at this juncture in time

It's He who hung by a nail our old garment in tow committed no crime

His only infraction was He loved us so much but still He was innocent

To make us worthy of the new garment for which we need only repent

Off with the worn out tattered Cloth of lingering past deeds good or bad

Rid the life that held us captured in the ethereal existence we once had

Slip into that new garment custom and tailored made with you in mind

Clothed in the unique fabric made with love, grace and His mercy entwined

Mark 2:21 "No one sews a patch of unshrunk cloth on an old garment. If they do, the new piece will pull away from the old, making the tear worse.

Listening

Lord I only want to hear

From you in all that I do

Let your voice become louder

Drowning out all background clamor

I have to have your direction

To be directed by only you

For my every decision

Knowing you will guide me right

Following the lead with You at the head

Hearing You whisper oh so sweet

Sweetly with love never intense

Trying to hear any word from You

A whisper loud enough yet still calming

Plainly spoken for the heart to comprehend

A wave of peace and calm hearing Your love

Still listening and hearing what You have to say

My child, I love you

Looking For My Father

Been thinking strongly about how much
I missed growing up without my father.
I know my life would be so different had
He lived during my formative years
My children might not be my children as they are now
My husband probably would not be the one of my choice.
A life filled with other experiences both bad and good.
But most of all I would have had the nurturing
That only a Daddy could give his special girl
A father prepares a daughter for a husband
By showing her how a man should treat her
This can be by giving her princess status
Or just being daddy's special little girl
A father provides her with a gentle touch
A soft rebuke not damaging her self-worth
Missed that daughter/daddy relationship
Wish I had heard it wish I heard it for myself
Who knows how we might have enjoyed
Those special times of encouragement, conversation
Telling me how beautiful I was and how I could achieve
Anything and everything I set my mind to do.
Life is for me to discover and live it to the fullest
That's what I believe my dad would have said
But while looking for my father my daddy
I was found by the Lord instead

Love Me More

Who can love me more than me

When I don't know to love me as much as I should

And don't love me as much as I possibly could

There is one who has all love all that I need

Even when love in my heart I don't feed

Even when I am not loving like I would me

Even when I allow others to taint what I see

Allowing them to take advantage of love I give

But this can't be the way that love is to live

Change must begin and end with love for me

Loving me as I should the way it has to be

Loving me more than just a little bit

Totally committed to love me because that's it

The Lord loves me more no questions asked

I must be obedient to His love commands

Loving the creature, He created which is me

Since that is the way this God given love should be

Loving me because I am worthy of the love

Sacrificing His love from His throne above

Make it So

It will be but you have to say so

What you say it is, is

But not without permission

Speak it so life comes and remains

I am because I say so

I am from my mouth

Words speak volumes

Make sure the volume is loud

Always keep the words flowing

Life will pour out

Life to the vision

Do not let it slip

I am, I am

I am what I say

Words from the heart fill my mouth

Make it so and so it is

Morning Sings Life

Morning came and I heard the first signs of life

A bird singing his song of the day effortless, no strife

The sound reminded me of the life that is in you

Laid back and relaxed though trouble pursues

Able to handle what is thrust at your feet

With courage and strength knowing this you can beat

Admiration is yours for the care you have given

The first morning song sings the life you are living

Move by it

We move by

Strength to Strength

Glory to Glory

Victory to Victory

We also move from

Test to Test

Trial to Trial

Grace to Grace

Mercy to Mercy

Seems impossible

Disconnected but interrelated

Intertwined feeding off each other

Test bring Strength

Trial becomes Glory

All results in Victory

By God's Grace and Jesus blood washed Mercy

New Life Today

A new life is before you with no regrets from the past

A chance to do something new only this time it will last

An opportunity to do something new different and unique

Endeavor to reach for higher heights more variety to seek

Seek not to entangle and intertwine without first much thought

Without the wisdom from above strife and troubles are brought

This journey can be done by yourself but never ever alone

He will always be with you as you make your way to His Throne

No More Insanity

Round and round in a circle seeing the same scenery

Meeting the same people, at the same time, same place

Saying the same words with the same emphasis

The same things done anticipating another outcome

Insanity makes it normal not realizing it is nuts

Long time nothing has changed

You and the situation all frozen in the moment

One day the same as the last – motionless in time

Change will never happen without a change

Try something new do something in an innovative way

Release the old for a new day has come

No more insanity, embrace the coming of ultimate contentment

The cycle has been broken replaced by sane decisions

Freshness – new sight – ears hearing soft

Sounds of sweet liberation

Insanity is doing things the same way and

Expecting different results

Sanity is doing different things and experiencing new life.

Much better

Not About You

There will be no self-promotion done in this vessel.

Yes, I said vessel which holds the Spirit

If the agenda is not the Lords, it will not prosper.

Would the Lord actually operate in this manner?

That is to say; he wants, requires, ask for no less than

Or more than complete surrender of all man's will

Not just requested of some while it seems others will slip

Through the cracks and attempt to skate pass what's right

I am confused are there two sets of standards in place

With some who have chosen to follow the required ones.

We all have the same standards to live by no change in that.

But some elect to turn a deaf or closed ear to the true word.

Can't I exalt or push my own agenda or anointing

To promote the gifts and talents the Lord as placed in me.

In doing so, would that help to lift the name of Jesus?

No, I cannot exalt self - no self-promoting agendas because

The anointing is not for me.

It is not for you.

It is not for me.

It is for God

Plan

Make sure to plan

But plan on the sure thing being done

God is the sure option

Opt not in your own plan

If God is not the architect of the plan

Acknowledge the master plan

Plan the master stand

When time have been accomplished

Season has ripened

Harvest will come forth

Stay in plan

Maintain your position

Wait patiently on time

Price of Sacrifice

Leadership has a price sacrifice is the cost
Strength comes from experience; it cost to be the boss
We all must pay the price our own cross to bear
Let the past push us forward, the past can't stay there
Run into the future with our heads held high
Those who went before us not in vain did they died
As we move to the top, a hand reaches back to another
The efforts made propel us ahead, no dream will we smother
All for a purpose to bring the world hope to achieve
One thing is required, in God we must believe
That unity is possible; freedom is now in our hand
Moving with the flow of God, a vision of the Promised Land
Elated with tremendous prospects our children can aspire to
Trusting in the Ultimate One that anything we can, we will do
Fostering His Glory, the love for us again He has shown
Showing forth His sovereign power, His plan be known
Destiny will be carried out no matter what hinders the progress
Struggles and setbacks now put aside for the promise of sweet rest
Rest in the realization that only He is in complete control
As long as we put the true Word first, everything else He will bestow
Believe my brother, have faith my sister, too
Putting our trust in Jesus, our heart after His heart is pursued

Dedicated to President Barack H. Obama

Reach Back

The time it takes to put me down

You could have been lifting me up

That mentality that exist that says

That your existence is better than mine

As one reaches the top

A hand comes down to another

As we push from the bottom

Reward well done my brother

As we reach

Ensuring the chain is not broken

Keep it intact

Effort benefits all

All win, not only one token

Be it woman or man

Regardless of shade

As you go up others should do the same

That is how success for all made

Say What

What do I say to this?
If God be for you
He is more than the world
Nothing can stand in your way
Nevertheless, the Lord has to be first
Will you change or will it be He
This change has to start with you
Love needs to be in you for you
If not the health of His love is not
Love yourself as well as your neighbor
Caressing the Lord, the Most High
None can take place of your first Love
Determine who that is then pursue
Must live with the choice made
Time is running out none to spare
Care should be taken soul is at stake
Cannot continue to write about
Failed relationships
Nothing gained but heartache
Heartache cannot be the choice
Joy in the Lord is the end result

Set the Atmosphere

Enter into His gates with thanksgiving
Into His courts with praise
As you enter into the doors, we are there to greet
With a handshake or hug with kindness we will meet
A show of love through a smile we invite
Sincerely wanting you to find some insight
Knowing you are not here by happenstance
But this is your day your time for deliverance
Now we usher you in to be blessed in His presence
We seat you so you can take full advantage
Where the Lord is there is liberty
To hear His anointed word that makes souls free
You have been strategically placed for your breakthrough
At the altar with love and concern, we cover you
To give the prophet a drink is to receive gain
To wipe his brow allows his strength to remain
We must realize that no position in the church is too small
But with our whole heart and intensity we answer our call
The call to servant hood is the best position there can be
To humble yourself to used and give Him all your abilities
For the Lord is well able to meet all your wants and needs
And with a surrendered spirit He will save you indeed.
Let us honor and respect those who seek to serve Him well
And ask for the will of God the Lord of every detail

Shades of Gray

With God, it is either black or white
In life there's shades of gray which makes the difference
With some people action speaks louder than words
With others the words speak volume initiating action
This is one of those gray areas shading life
The spiritual realm has right or wrong yet
You can either do this for one result
Or, do that for just the opposite effect
Life has the same promise but those clouded areas
Grayness falls between what is clear as crystal white or black
It is that which is allowable or not very sure what it means
Words are important for me telling exactly what I need to do
No clue is given with words that are left unsaid not spoken
One of those gray places leading into the deeper shades
Why drift any further aimlessly accepting whatever it won't do
It is like a cloudy day and you know the sun is shining somewhere
Shining but hidden by the gray clouds brightness is elsewhere
Obstructing the sunniness day, you have ever seen, hope to again
Between you and heaven is that gray area having to see the hues
The gray areas are full of confusion blurred and undefined
Not able to distinguish light from darkness for it's a mixed array
Who knows which clouds are what's very real, barely real, somewhat real
Not real no matter what shade hence that sunless but not so dark day

Still She Longs

Still she longs for all she does not know

The promise of that blessing which could be

All she knows is something better on the horizon

Makes her stare in the distant images faint but clearer

Coming into focus the more she looks ahead

Still she longs for familiar though new is expected

The more she waits more encouraged she is

If wait is this extensive, imagine the gain

Did not ask but patience makes her stronger

A voice says not much longer endurance will pay off

Not much longer seems an impossible task

Hold out try to last reward will come fast

Stills she longs, not for what slipped by

Longs for the promise, what is promised, will be

Suddenly I Was in Prayer

It was not my intention in fact
I was in the midst of something else
Suddenly the spirit took control so I decided to flow with it
Did I have the time, yes and most definitely the opportunity
It was just that it was not my intention to pray at that time
I had a mind and plan to be doing something else instead
Suddenly I was in prayer, much needed, timely and intense prayer
If I was trying to reach someone else, I would have been persistent
Suddenly I was in prayer and someone was trying to reach me
Relentless and intense instantly I was there – so I flowed with it
It was graceful and not much talking on my part, time for listening
To hear what the Lord had to say to me – No interruptions – time to hear
Putting everything aside – to pick it up later – I was in the right place
The words were reassuring, giving peace to the mind and soul
Suddenly I was in the midst of prayer – Fluently, completely there
Answers to this and answers to that giving surety He knows and cares
Even answers to those things unspoken only in the heart – still unsaid
Encouraging words and words of instruction and words to give it all over
Not holding anything back – totally and completely surrender releasing,
giving surrender, yielding, submitting, giving up and giving in,
Laying it all down at His feet saying yes because with
Amen it is the only answer - aye and amen

Suddenly I Was in Prayer Continued

Following to lead and leading to following –more is less multiplied
Hear what the Spirit is saying, refreshing like rain on a hot summer day
So easily the letting loose was made – trusting only to be made free
Trusting and believing because suddenly I was in prayer

Strength in Numbers

We can be strong all by ourselves

The number One is valid alone

But the bible says where there are two or three

United in His name agreeing can get the job done

For uniting in mind with a common goal

Nothing is impossible we have the reward

Look at the people of Babel wanting to reach heaven

With the material, tools and labor at hand

Only God could disturb their effort and plan

But look what they could have accomplished

There would exist a stairway to heaven the easy way

One can put a thousand to flight

But two can do ten times as much

Although it may not take an army to get it done

Just a few together we can accomplish anything

This Time

Many thoughts come to mind
Some bring joy and warm feelings
Others make you wonder
If life is really worth the struggle.
Then there are the ones
That makes you reflect on past events
Thinking if I could only live that one again
It would be different this time
This time there will a better outcome.
So, my advice to myself is to think twice
Maybe three times before acting
And this even to say
To ask the Source of all thought
What is the best course of action?
Then wait on His action plan
What is the sense creating a new process?
When there is already one in place
That you have not lived yet.
Every day there is a continuation
The established course of action
Set before your existence began
Will the plan work this time?
When the plan is only set for you.

Time and Seasons

There is a time and a season for all things a timely span
Winter into spring into summer into fall without help from man.
It is all a natural occurrence all in the plan.
We are born and we grow, mature if we can
God created us to use what He placed in our hand
What time is it for you?
There are seasons in our life where we are to accomplish
The plan of God set before us to complete we encompass
There are seasons for some people to be in our life
Maybe to help us along some of life's journey precise
But as seasons come to an end and a new one surface
So does their time hopefully to achieve its set purpose
Then there are the season people who come to teach
Show or give lessons either good or bad so to reach
Not to stay for long so try not to keep them around
For time may not be long to learn lessons again profound
Same lesson over and over again when once should be plenty
So make sure to use time given you wisely for lessons are many
Fulfilling your purpose and assignment to do them well
In time doing all of what life's lessons may entail
What time are you waiting for?

Ecclesiastes 3:1
To everything there is a season, and a time to every purpose under the
heaven

Touch Treasure

We said we want to be like Him

Do we really know what that means?

To touch the sensitivity of God

Always in His Presence

Live as He lives

Say what He says

Feel what He feels

Be who He is

See what He sees

Understand what He knows

Immersed in his anointing

Again to touch the consideration of God

Great sacrifice great anointing

Life never to be our own forever

No more I but Christ dwelling

To touch the heart of God touching all

We Have No Limits

Now is the time for us to gather
Together to work for cooperation instead of competition
We now have the power that we really had all the long
But now we vote in elections
We are greater than we think with
Nothing to stop us but us nothing at all
The day for equality has fully
Come and we have the right to participate in the process
The making of our country the making of
History the making of our future of us
Many helped to get us to this point the
Point of achieving a freedom a liberation
To be all that we can be and show
Our children that there no limits to their dreams
Their visions their potentials their
Desires their abilities or being whatever makes us strong
Age shouldn't stop us when many have
Started their dreams in the middle of life
Thinking you have nothing to offer
When your experience holds a wealth of knowledge
Witty ideas carefully planned ventures
Educated in one area but prepared you for different
We are scientists, lawyers, doctors,
Congresswomen, presidential candidates, writers
Many of us were the first to do it,
Jeannette Pickering Rankin first congresswoman who said

We Have No Limits Continued

She wouldn't be the last and she's not
For other firsts came after her, have to start somewhere
Shirley Chisholm the first black congresswoman
And presidential candidate started something
Started the inspiration that maybe
We can be the first to start something igniting potential
The first to encourage someone to go on and
Achieve more than you have, no envy
Just do better, do more, encouraging words,
Got your back kind of support you can do it
Had my firsts too and they started
Something, inspired others to do something do more
Be different for our journeys are not
The same, my path is not yours but still has to be traveled
Try it, for failure is in not ever attempting,
Reaching, starting the expedition of your dream
For rejection should only send you in another
Direction, not stopping the adventure
We are limitless in our abilities because
Most of us have not even achieved our total potential
There are songs not sang, books not read,
Inventions not used and foods not tasted yet
Don't let time and opportunities past us by
Without daring endeavoring making that first effort
Be the wind in someone's sail as you let
Someone else be the wind in yours, no jealousy
For every first either personal or corporate
Begins with the first step, step on step out, step in

What's Wrong with Today

Why not let Him lead the way?

Make up your mind to stay

Do what He wants what He say

He is the best no need to stray

Serve Him from the heart enemy at bay

At His feet your burdens can lay

Trusting God if your heart may

What's wrong with today

What's wrong with tonight

Why not let Him be your sight?

The way is narrow road is tight

Jesus says He is the shining light

The path was dark but now is bright

You can run this race with His might

He's there through the depth and height

The battle is the Lord's it's His fight

What's wrong with tonight

What's wrong with now

Time is getting short not much is found

Got to get it together all else is unsound

Escape what the enemy makes no rebound

To be in a God place making a glory sound

At the foot of the throne find us on safe ground

What's wrong with today, tonight or now

What is the Answer?

Will we ever know the whole story on this side of time?
Will it ever make sense… will the words ever really rhythm?
Will it be nay, aye, or this time wait?
Patience is wearing thin, nothing to date…
Standing still but running in place!
Moving but not going - still at a steady pace…
Can it be that the time to move has come and gone?
Hesitated or delayed just a little too long?
Did the door open but looking the wrong way?
Perhaps let hindrances, stalling tactics missed the day.
Eyes blinded by what the world has shown
Vision clouded looking in front, looking too long
Will the time, the moment, ever reappear?
How will I know when the moment is here?
Holding still to comfort and what is safe
Holding on to what I think is my place
Afraid to venture - scare to embrace…
Embrace what God says, "I must face"
Face with boldness the future with grace
Face the glory, let the past be erased
Leaving childhood, shelter of home…
Past practice, old habits, what was prone…?
Don't want to miss the blessing for me alone!
Lead me with Your Light, illuminate my path!
Direct along the strait the Way - You hath!
All roads are not the same or exact…
Mine will go this way, but the plan is intact…
The plan is still the plan has the same aim…
Refocus, realign having His mind, then yours is tamed!

You Stood Up

You stood up at a time not knowing what you would face

Boldly admitting it was time to fully enter this challenging race

Taking on the mantle passed on by your father's home going

With all the seeds planted, our prayers we both were sowing

What I am doing -what was I thinking, may have been your cry

Next question pondered may have been should I even try

God knew the timing was right and you were up the task

And He would always have your back if you would only ask

The Lord knew the when the why and the what for

When you stood up, The Lord became the Who, the open door

Your- go –to Man in time of indecision and even a little doubt

The One who says have faith in ME, I'll show you what I'm all about

Hear what the spirit is saying to you being the church

Your assignment, your purpose, your destiny it will be much

Not hard nor difficult for you have been equipped

All the tools are in place and He will not let you slip

Your companion for life is there right by your side

To do those things that are in her hands she will abide

You Stood Up Continued

Precious is your union strong is your love

Orchestrated and designed in heaven, heaven above

So, look to the hills from which cometh your aid

Seeing the future unfold with fortitude and faith the way is made

Stronger and stronger you will be as the tests and trials you tackle

Believing God for any and everything your fetters He will unshackle

Why Do They Hate My Son

Why do they hate my son?
What makes them think
They are doing the right thing?
He only came to redeem man from sin
The sin that first man let in
Why do they hate my son?
I am hearing all the lies they say
I never would have let this happen
If I could it wouldn't be this way
He is my first born He lived right near my heart
Why do they hate my son?
Watching them beat him and this is only the start
Seeing the blood, oh so much blood
His wounds are more than I can take
What could I say to this what words when
Not a complaining word would He make
Why do they hate my son?
The struggle of the cross is great
Who is there to help him with the weight?
And now He's at the cross
My child is hanging in front of me
His feet I will kiss
He lived to do His father's will
My first born child, my love I will miss
Why did they hate my son?
For the promise of his father
To rise again

www.ingramcontent.com/pod-product-compliance
Lightning Source LLC
Chambersburg PA
CBHW060429050426
42449CB00009B/2204